# The Oi

# Negotiator

# The One-hour Negotiator

BERGER

Pierre Casse

Illustrations by Berger

BUTTERWORTH
HEINEMANN

Butterworth-Heinemann
Linacre House, Jordan Hill, Oxford OX2 8DP
A division of Reed Educational and Professional Publishing Ltd

Ɑ A member of the Reed Elsevier plc group

OXFORD    BOSTON    JOHANNESBURG
MELBOURNE    NEW DELHI    SINGAPORE

First published 1992
Reprinted 1995, 1996

**British Library Cataloguing in Publication Data**
Casse, Pierre
  One-hour Negotiator
  I. Title
  658.4

ISBN 0 7506 0735 1

Printed in Great Britain by Hartnolls Ltd., Bodmin, Cornwall.

# Contents

# Introduction

## On your way to a negotiation...

This book is for business people – and busy people – who want to learn how to negotiate more effectively.

This book is simple and to the point. It does not beat around the bush. It presents some **key messages** on how to be a more effective negotiator.

The text is based on one assumption:

You, the reader, are en route to a negotiation. You have precisely **one hour** to review basic negotiating principles and prepare yourself for a successful bargaining session.

That's what the book is all about. A summary of negotiation essentials that you can review and memorize in sixty minutes. So if you are in a plane or train, just relax... go ahead, refresh your mind... and **enjoy**.

Now, if you don't have even one hour – don't bother. Don't even start reading. Just stick to these **three golden rules:**

1. Be aware of **what** you are doing

2. Be aware of the **impact** your words and actions have on others

3. If you are not getting what you want with your words and actions – try **different** words, different actions. What you are doing is not working. Do something else.

Good negotiators have three things in common. They give themselves plenty of options if things get sticky. They are flexible enough to use those options. And their minds are quick enough to adjust to the fast-changing requirements of the negotiating situation.

This book has only one objective: to help you be a better negotiator, and get more of what you want from other people. There is no question that success belongs to those who are able to use their **negotiating imagination**.

**Good Luck!**

# CHAPTER 1

**A quick review:
questions to be asked...**

**...and answered**

# Question 1

## *Are you a negotiator?*

✘ What is a negotiator?

✘ Why do we negotiate?

✘ When was my last negotiation?

✘ What have I learned?

✘ How do I feel about negotiation?

**Of course you are a negotiator!**

**Any doubt?**

**Check it out!**

This is a simple test. Look at the picture[1] on this page and make up a story from it. Use your imagination, without constraint. Let your mind roam. Be spontaneous.

Try to keep your story in your mind. If you don't think you can remember it, write it down.

When you have finished, turn the page to see if you are – or are not – a negotiator.

---

[1] This picture is part of the classic T.A.T. (Thematic Apperception Test). It is unclear on purpose.

# Checklist to see if you are a negotiator

In your story, do you have people (check if appropriate):

☐ arguing about something?        ☐ enjoying a fight?

☐ making a point?                 ☐ compromising

☐ rejecting an idea?              ☐ pushing and getting upset?

☐ looking thoughtful?             ☐ teaching others?

☐ leaving the room?               ☐ trying to persuade others?

If you checked all of these items, there is no doubt that you are a negotiator. In fact, you already know quite a lot about the subject.

If you checked 5-9 of these items, you are still a negotiator. But, apparently, you believe that negotiation is something you are not permanently involved in.

If you checked four or less of these items, you are perhaps trying to convince yourself that negotiation is really not your business... but **you are wrong! As the next page will prove...**

Whatever your story is, it should demonstrate that

1. All human interactions are characterized by some kind of negotiation between (or among) people trying to give to and take from one another.

## Exchange[1]

2. Negotiation exists when somebody is trying to influence another person through the use of various media.

## Persuasion[2]

3. Intra-negotiation is a fact of life – the struggle within your own mind every time you have to make a decision.

## Decision[3]

By the way, **negotiation** is the process by which at least two parties with different perception, needs, motivations try to agree on a matter of mutual interest.

---

[1] Karrass. C.L. *Give and Take*. New York: Thomas Y. Crowell Co., 1974.
[2] Bellenger, L. *La persuasion*. Paris: P.U.F., 1985.
[3] Janis, I.L. and Mann L., *Decision Making*. New York: The Free Press, 1977.

# Question 2

## *What kind of a negotiator are you?*

Take one minute to reflect on the kind of negotiator you are.

**GENTLE?**

**TOUGH?**

**WELL PREPARED?**

**AGGRESSIVE?**

**FLEXIBLE?**

# Being a negotiator?

## *An action list*

The real question is: "What kind of negotiator are you?" Go back to the story you imagined from the picture on page 7. Can you see if you are the kind of person who:

1. Enjoys negotiation very much. (Do people in your story laugh, smile, and enjoy the process?)

2. Trusts himself and others. (Do you find anything related to trust in your story?)

3. Is optimistic about negotiation. (Does your imaginary negotiation have a happy ending?)

## Keep in mind these three negotiation factors:

☛ **Enjoyment and relaxation**

☛ **Trust and self-confidence**

☛ **Optimism and expectation**

**All right, you are a negotiator...**

But the question now is: **"How good are you?"**

# Question 3

*What are your key negotiating strengths and weaknesses?*

| **Strengths** | **Weaknesses** |
|---|---|
| 1. ............................... | 1. ................................ |
| 2. ............................. | 2. ............................... |
| 3. .............................. | 3. ................................ |

Document your negotiating strengths and weaknesses with events that you experienced in the last three years:

✎ ....................................................................................

........................................................................................

........................................................................................

........................................................................................

........................................................................................

........................................................................................

The first thing a good negotiator has to do is to recognize when s/he is in a negotiation.

In your judgment, which of these words characterize a negotiation situation? What is your definition of negotiation?

| | |
|---|---|
| ❐ challenge | ❐ expectations |
| ❐ opportunity | ❐ agreement |
| ❐ exchange | ❐ give |
| ❐ confrontation | ❐ argue |
| ❐ compromise | ❐ persuasion |
| ❐ wants | ❐ parties |
| ❐ needs | ❐ pressure |

Read again the definition of negotiation and go back to your selection of words to see if they fit:

> *"Negotiation is the process by which at least two parties with different assumptions, needs and expectations try to agree on a matter of mutual interest."*

Reflect on your own definition of negotiation and try to identify somebody that you admire as a good negotiator (Role Modelling). What do you learn from him or her?

**Lessons from others:** 1. ...........................................................

2. ...........................................................

3. ...........................................................

# A reminder

**Three key things to keep in mind:**

## 1. We negotiate all the time

Negotiation is an ongoing process. It is informal and goes on all the time. For instance, I negotiate when I:

- ✔ wake up in the morning
- ✔ talk to my children
- ✔ meet with my boss
- ✔ discuss with my friend
- ✔ go to a restaurant...

## 2. Everything is negotiable

This does not mean that you will "win" all the time. But you can always try to get as much as you can out of any situation, including critical issues like your destiny, your health… even your own death.

## 3. Negotiation can be learned

Some are better than others at the negotiating "game". And yet, yes, everybody can improve his or her ability to negotiate through the acquisition of knowledge, skills and experiences.

# Assess now your ability to negotiate:

## 1. Knowledge

How much do you know about negotiation theories?

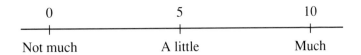

(How many books on negotiation have you read in the last 12 months?)

## 2. Skills

How good are you at practising negotiation skills and techniques?

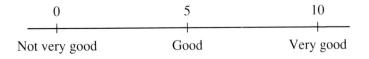

(When did you last participate in a negotiation workshop?)

## 3. Experiences

What have you learned from your last negotiation?

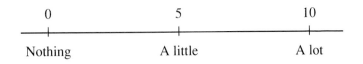

(When was it? How successful were you? Why?)

# Your negotiating strengths and weaknesses

According to C.L. Karrass[1], successful negotiators have features which distinguish them from average or poor negotiators. Take a moment to compare yourself to the profile of a good negotiator:

    **1.**    Negotiators with high **aspirations** win high rewards.

**Comments:**

Do you believe in yourself, and in the "cause" you are fighting for? Do you expect a lot of yourself – and, honestly, do you see yourself getting it?

    **2.**    Negotiators who make small **concessions** succeed more.

**Comments:**

Less effective negotiators tend to concede more at the start of the negotiation than toward its end. Are you aware of your own "concession patterns"?

    **3.**    **Power** and **negotiating skills** both contribute to success in negotiation.

**Comments:**

Having more power than your opposite number is no guarantee of success in negotiations. Power is a greater factor in a negotiation's outcome when the negotiators are unskilled.

---

Karrass, C.L., *The Negotiating Game*. New York: Thomas Y. Crowell Co., 1974.

# Take one more minute to check on your negotiating effectiveness

# Question 4

## *Are you ready for the negotiation ahead?*

Keep in mind that a negotiation is always a new challenge:

- ☛ You are different from the last negotiation
- ☛ The people you are going to negotiate with are also different
- ☛ The issues are new
- ☛ The context is not the same

**It is a challenge!**

# READINESS is the key to successful negotiation

Let's assume that you are on your way to a negotiation. Let's see how READY you are.

Read each item and check the appropriate answer. Take no more than one minute to do this.

| | Absolutely | Not quite | Not at all |
|---|---|---|---|
| | 5 | 3 | 1 |
| 1. I know what my negotiating objectives are | 5 | 3 | 1 |
| 2. I am aware of what the other party is looking for | 5 | 3 | 1 |
| 3. I have a negotiation plan | 5 | 3 | 1 |
| 4. I have explored various ways to tackle the key negotiation issues | 5 | 3 | 1 |
| 5. I have already decided which issues I will – and will not – compromise | 5 | 3 | 1 |
| 6. I have gathered information on the other party's background | 5 | 3 | 1 |

| | Absolutely | Not quite | Not at all |
|---|:---:|:---:|:---:|
| | **5** | **3** | **1** |
| **7.** I am prepared for potential deadlocks | **5** | **3** | **1** |
| **8.** I am ready to cope with stress | **5** | **3** | **1** |
| **9.** I am fully familiar with my negotiation "dossier" | **5** | **3** | **1** |
| **10.** I know what my negotiating strengths and weaknesses are | **5** | **3** | **1** |

Add up your score, and then identify your strengths and weaknesses in negotiating using these guidelines:

**10 ⇨ 20**   Let's face it – you are not very well prepared for the coming negotiation. If you are good at improvising, you might get out without too much harm. If you are not, you still might get lucky – but don't be surprised if you not only don't get what you hoped for, but get "taken to the cleaners" as well.

**20 ⇨ 40**   You are basically all right, but there are still some key areas to work on in order to be on the safe side. Advice: go back to those items where you scored **1** and **3**. See what you can do to reinforce your preparation.

**40 ⇨ 50**   You are very ready indeed! We can predict with confidence that your negotiation will be a success.

Go back to the questionnaire and see now where you are a bit weak. Think about what you can do to improve. Now!…

**Check again with the checklist below.**

## Criteria for effective negotiation: ACTION LIST

**To be successful, you must check your readiness on these points:**

| Negotiation content | Negotiation process |
|---|---|
| **1.** Good knowledge of what's at stake | **1.** High expectations |
| **2.** Clear idea about objectives | **2.** Good knowledge of other party: <br> – *background* <br> – *priorities* <br> – *action plan* |
| **3.** Priorities selected | **3.** Acquisition of key negotiation skills |
| **4.** Negotiation plan ready …and readiness to adjust plan if needed | **4.** Ability to work under stress |
| **5.** Ready to document key arguments | **5.** Power and authority to negotiate |

**Success in negotiation is closely related
to two prerequisites:**

☛ **Know yourself**

☛ **Know the party you negotiate with**

# Question 5

## *How well do you know the people you are going to negotiate with?*
### *(Negotiation intelligence)*

Japanese business people take an average of one year to prepare themselves for a foreign negotiation? What about you?

    ✗  **How familiar are you with the other party?**

    ✗  **Do they know you?**

    ✗  **How critical is this negotiation for them?**

Have you done your homework? Do you have all the information about the other party to your negotiation that you need to negotiate effectively? Or are you missing some key pieces of information?

For example, do you know:

1.    What they expect from the negotiation (objectives)
2.    Who is going to negotiate (number, experience, skills, profile, power)
3.    Their strengths and weaknesses

4. What they know about you

5. If they are under pressure from:
   - their boss
   - their clients
   - others

6. If there is a time constraint

7. What their feelings about the negotiation are

8. What's at stake for them

9. What would turn them on… or off

10. When it is important for you to **match** or **mismatch** them (see the next page)

# Negotiation guidelines

## *Matching*

**Matching** is the process by which you adjust your behaviour to the other party's style or habits so that you get his or her attention, a positive reaction and – eventually – an agreement.

## *Mismatching*

**Mismatching** is the process by which you act exactly opposite to the other party's behavioural patterns. It triggers a negative reaction, withdrawal and eventually a disagreement.

## Illustrations of matching behaviour in negotiation

1. Speaking at the same speed as the other party
2. Using the same tone
3. Making the same gestures
4. Making brief statements, if that's the style of the other party
5. Touching, sitting, drinking, listening, expressing ourselves – the same way as the other party
6. Taking time working on the agenda if this is important for the other party

7. Focusing on results (with action-oriented negotiators)

8. Getting acquainted and responding to social demands

9. Brainstorming and playing with ideas to meet the conceptual needs of the other negotiators

10. Checking the facts if this is what they want…

(**Mismatching** behaviour is exactly the reverse of the above list).

# It is critical to know the type of negotiator you are dealing with

## *Four basic types of negotiators*[1]
(Who is your "opponent"?)

Let's have a look at the basic **types** of negotiators. There is a good chance you will meet and try to negotiate with each different type – if you haven't done so already.

**The Crook**

**The Professional**

---

[1] If interested in the subject, read "The Basic Laws of Human Stupidity", by C.M. Cipolla, *Whole Earth Review*, Spring 1987.

**The Stupid**

**The Naive**

There is a mixture of the four types in each individual. We are all a bit crook, stupid, naive and professional. It depends on the situation, the subject, the other party, the time...

See next page for a description of the four negotiators' profiles:

## The CROOK negotiator

### Pointers

It isn't always easy to identify a crook negotiator. You must be aware that there is no question in his mind that he should win – and you should lose. He wants to get everything. He deserves it. You don't. He will use all the means at his disposal to achieve his objective.

There are different types of crooks. You should know them:

- ✔ The **upfront crook negotiator**. He tells you right at the outset what he wants and where he stands.

- ✔ The **smart crook negotiator**. He does not tell you anything and sometimes it is only when the negotiation is over that you realize that you have been had.

- ✔ The **devious crook negotiator**. He will wait until the end of the negotiation to reveal himself and get you. You will resent it, but… too late. He is a great manipulator.

### Tips

Always try to determine the intention of your opposite number. If you believe that s/he is a "crook", you have two choices:

- ✌ Break the negotiation, or
- ✌ Set up the rules of the negotiation in such a way that you cannot be exploited.

### Recommended behaviour

Be attentive and on your guard. Watch, listen, ask questions and protect yourself by using safeguards.

# The PROFESSIONAL negotiator

## Pointers

You can feel it right at the start: the other party is a pro! He knows **what** you are negotiating – your goals and his – and he knows **how** to go about getting what he wants. He has the knowledge, the power and, most important, the skills needed to negotiate effectively.

Very quickly you discover that he knows a lot about you. His moves are well-planned. By and large, he tries to define the final negotiating position so that both parties win as much as possible.

## Tips

In most cases, it is to your advantage to cooperate with a professional negotiator since he is looking for a win-win situation. Depending on your own strength, adjust the level of your own trust to profit from the professional's basic orientation. But remain vigilant. It doesn't take much for a professional negotiator to become a **crook**!

## Recommended behaviour

Go along. Participate. Lead and accept being led. There is a good chance that the outcome of the negotiation will come out of the **synergy**[1] you will experience during the interaction with the other party.

---

*Synergy* is the ability to produce together what you cannot produce as individuals. It means new solutions, new ways to look at the issues. It is based on the use of your negotiating imagination.

## The STUPID negotiator

### Pointers

He is stupid because he is going to make you both lose. Whatever you do, he will act in such a way that you cannot (and he cannot) win. It is a deadlock situation. It can also be dangerous in the sense that if he is drowning, he can take you with him.

### Tips

It is important for you to detect as quickly as possible if the other party is

    ✌    As stupid as he claims to be.

    ✌    Stupid for rational or irrational reasons.

If he is really stupid, forget it. You are not going to get anywhere. If he is pretending to be stupid, see what you can do to change the situation – as recommended below.

### Recommended behaviour

To change the situation, you must know what's behind the other party's behaviour. For instance:

| | | |
|---|---|---|
| If he is afraid to lose | ⇨ | **reassure him** |
| If he doesn't understand | ⇨ | **explain** |
| If he feels threatened by you | ⇨ | **be low key and considerate** |

32

## The NAIVE negotiator

### Pointers

You will recognize him very quickly. He is not prepared, does not know what the issue is and trusts you to a point where he is ready to give you anything you want.

With a naive negotiator you **win** and he **loses**. It's effortless. You direct and he follows. Enjoy, but… be careful.

### Tips

YES. Be careful, because the naive negotiator may be:

- ✌ Not as naive as you think

- ✌ Hiding something

- ✌ Agreeing to what you want because he has something else in mind (a bigger fish…)

- ✌ Obeying instructions from his boss to give in, so that… you will be trapped

- ✌ Ready to lose now because he knows he will win in the long term

### Recommended behaviour

Probe gently. Try to discover what's behind the naiveté of the other party. Move step by step. Check if the other party is **really** lost, of if there is something else going on. If he is really lost, set up a win-win negotiation – which is in the interest of both of you. If he is faking, watch out for the hidden agenda… and the trap.

# And finally

A last hint on how to gather information on the other negotiating party:

- ☞ Get all written documents about him or her
- ☞ Talk to people who know him
- ☞ Try to set up a pre-negotiation meeting before your first formal negotiation session.

Still assuming you are going to negotiate soon, can you:

- ✗ Visualize him?
- ✗ Determine his likes and dislikes?
- ✗ Identify what his most sensitive areas are?

Work on your **negotiation intelligence**!

# Basic knowledge about the other negotiator:

**Who am I negotiating with?** Now, answer these questions:

1. What does s/he want?
2. How important is it to him/her
3. Does s/he want it **now** – or later?
4. How much is s/he ready to give to get it?
5. Can s/he get it from someone other than you?

## And now, rehearse:[1]

**Phase 1**  Outline, as realistically as possible, the profile of the other party.

**Phase 2**  Define his/her negotiating position as intelligently as you can. You want to make **your** job as challenging as possible.

**Phase 3**  Set up rules for the negotiation (how many people, time, setting…).

**Phase 4**  "Play" the negotiation (as many times as needed).

**Phase 5**  Debrief the exercise and learn from it.

---

[1] If you didn't have time to rehearse, do it (now) in your mind. Put yourself in the other party's shoes, negotiate against yourself, switch roles… and learn from your fantasies by looking at them closely.

**Use your fantasies to visualize what could happen**

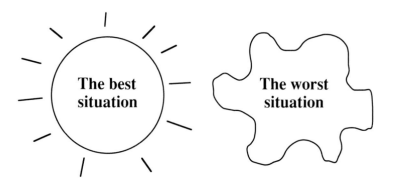

**Take one minute to answer the following question:**

*At the end of the negotiation, would you be delighted if (what?)*

✎

1. .......................................................................
   .......................................................................

2. .......................................................................
   .......................................................................

3. .......................................................................
   .......................................................................

# A quick review: Questions to be asked

## *Summary*

A few key questions must be raised before going to your negotiation:

1.  What kind of a negotiator are you? (Strengths? Weaknesses?)

2.  What about "them"? Do you know the people you are going to negotiate with? Their strengths? Their weaknesses?

3.  Are you convinced that **everything is negotiable?**

4.  Check your **assumptions** before entering the negotiation?

5.  Are you really ready for your next negotiation?

**… and do you remember the types of negotiators?**

# CHAPTER 2

# A life case study to sharpen your negotiation mind

# Life case study

Sharpen your negotiation ability by reading the short case study below and by answering the following questions:

*Assuming that you are the Swedish CEO of Automat International:*

1. What is your diagnosis of the situation in Belgium? (What's wrong?) Is this a negotiation?

2. How would you handle this negotiation? (What do you do? How?)

3. What do you learn from this life case? (See comments at the end of the case)

# Automat International

"What do we do now" the CEO of Automat International (Process Automation Control) in Stockholm, Sweden, asked the team of managers he had invited to discuss the critical situation of the marketing subsidiary in Belgium.

"It is difficult to know what is going on when you are so far away," responded a manager.

One way or another, a plan to improve profitability was needed as soon as possible.

## Background

The Belgian marketing subsidiary had been established in 1977. It had had a good start, but in 1983 Stockholm managers noticed that turnover was not growing as well as it could. It seemed that the sales of systems, which represented about 75% of the business, were not developing as expected.

In 1984, Systems and Instruments were divided into two divisions at both the factory and marketing levels. Three managers (all Belgian) were involved at that time, Jan Schothorst, Pete van der Laan and Jacob Verdoren. (See Figure 1, The Partial Subsidiary Structure).

**Figure 1:**
*The partial subsidiary structure*

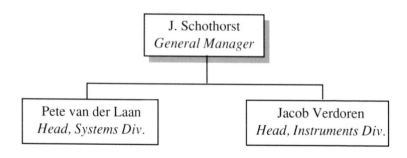

J. Schothorst was the Managing Director responsible for the supervision of Pete van der Laan, the newly appointed head of the Systems Division. Jacob Verdoren, the former head of the Sales Division, was now in charge of the Instruments Division, considered less prestigious than Systems company-wide because instruments was a more stable market and therefore had slower growth.

**Personality Profiles**

**Jan Schothorst**, Managing Director
Belgian, 50 years old.

- Bureaucratic
- Nervous and tense at work
- Reluctant to take risk
- Wants to know everything
- Goes by the book
- Follows the budget
- Nice, gentle, warm, soft when with people
- Has been in the business for a long time
- Good professional
- Does not take initiative
- Not very supportive of team members

**Pete van der Laan**, Head of the Systems Division
Belgian, 39 years old

- Ambitious
- Good academic credentials
- Analytical
- Aggressive, pushy
- Lacks self-confidence (uses others to back up his ideas)
- Direct and forceful
- Has strong personal motives (his career first)
- Good "manipulator"
- Looks younger than he actually is
- Competitive

**Jacob Verdoren**, Head of the Instruments Division
(Former Sales Manager for joint division)
Belgian, 49 years old

- Down-to-earth
- Good field experience
- Business oriented
- Extrovert
- Suspicious at times
- Good at networking (a lot of personal contacts)
- Guarded
- Excited at times
- Sometimes lacks self-confidence.

## The Situation

The subsidiary's performance did not improve after the split. It seemed that Jan Schothorst was not able to control the situation, and in 1985, Stockholm began to look for another person to take over as Managing Director. Promoting the new Systems Division head, Pete van der Laan, to the top position was being considered.

This information leaked out to the potential candidate and he proceeded to collect information on Mr. Schothorst's performance and relay it to Stockholm. At the same time, he teamed up with Jacob Verdoren who also did not appreciate the Managing Director.

Meanwhile, the Managing Director refused to attend key systems sales meetings with customers. In addition, Jacob Verdoren, head of the Instruments Division, was trying to sell systems without informing his counterpart who, at the same time, recruited several sales people without having a plan (the increase should have been more gradual and should have been started sooner).

Costs were increasing and the performance of the subsidiary continued to decline.

The worsening situation continued throughout 1985. In January 1986, several people from Stockholm visited the Belgian subsidiary and met with each of the managers. An outside consultant, a psychologist, conducted interviews with the three people concerned. As a result of the discussions, in March 1986 the Managing Director was fired, the first time in Automat International's history. A Swede named Eriksen was appointed as the new director for a six month period.

## The New Director

The premise under which Mr. Eriksen accepted this position was that Mr. van der Laan would eventually succeed him as Managing Director. He already knew Mr. Verdoren with whom he got along well. However, it soon was apparent that the head of the Systems Division did not want to cooperate with the new Managing Director. Mr. van der Laan would get his sales group to support his ideas and then use his sales people as leverage against the Managing Director's ideas. Mr. van der Laan also refused to work with Mr. Verdoren.

In November 1986, Mr. van der Laan and Mr. Verdoren went through some testing to determine the most suitable candidate for the position of Managing Director. Mr. Verdoren cooperated, but Mr. van der Laan strongly objected to the test which he claimed was illegal.

The subsidiary's profitability was not at an acceptable level at the end of 1986. Stockholm decided that the subsidiary should report every month to the CEO directly. In March 1987, the CEO met with Eriksen and van der Laan to discuss their conflicting views regarding the future. Mr. van der Laan expressed confidence that sales would soon improve whereas Mr. Eriksen argued that there would be no improvement and suggested that the number of systems engineers be reduced. He also recommended that the quality of systems sales people be evaluated.

"So, gentlemen, what do we do?" the head of the Automat Process Automation Group again asked.

## Comments

Obviously the CEO had to start with J. Schothorst and first learn what had been wrong with him.

That diagnosis would have led to a series of key questions regarding the profiles of the people the company head office had to negotiate with:

1. What about their cultural backgrounds?
2. Why the lack of communication and cooperation?
3. What about the key players' respective strengths and weaknesses?
4. Was the psychologist a good idea?
5. What is the bottom line problem?

A close look at the personality profiles and the overal situation in 1986 leads us to believe that some drastic measures were required and that the negotiation should have been quick, to the point and non-participatory. A Swedish manager (different from Mr. Eriksen) should have been appointed for at least three years.

Do you agree?

Let's move on to the analysis of the critical negotiation steps. The question is:

## How do we manage negotiation?

**The three critical steps in negotiation are:**

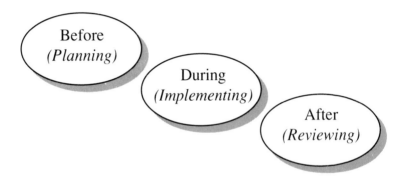

# CHAPTER 3

## The negotiation planning step

# *Before*

## Planning the negotiation requires three key tasks:

***Task 1:*** **Set up your GOALS**

A negotiating goal is what you want to achieve.

***Task 2:*** **Decide on your STRATEGY**

A strategy is how you are going to reach your goal.

***Task 3:*** **Clarify the PROCESS**

The process is how the negotiation unfolds according to some group dynamic laws.

### An integrated negotiation model

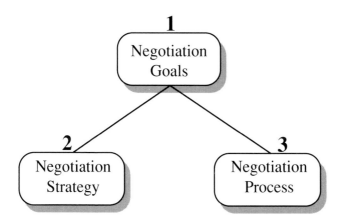

# 1.  Negotiation goal

A negotiation goal is what you expect to get out of the negotiation. This is why you negotiate in the first place. It is absolutely critical to all negotiations.

There are two types of goals:

## Ideal goal

- This is what you intend to get if everything goes well

- It is an ideal objective. (It is the maximum you can get)

- It is an opening goal. (You start at the top)

## Bottom line goal

- This is the minimum you will accept

- It is a walk away position

- You use it near the end of the negotiation.

## Questions for the negotiator:

✗ Do you know what your ideal goal is?

✗ What about your walk away position or bottom line?

✗ Can you answer again the following question:
   *"At the end of the negotiation, I'll be very happy if…"*

✗ Do you know the other party's ideal and bottom line goals?

# Once More:

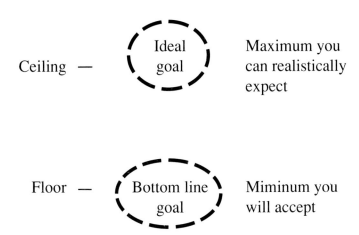

Ceiling — **Ideal goal**    Maximum you can realistically expect

Floor — **Bottom line goal**    Miminum you will accept

## Tips for the negotiator:

Effective negotiators have a tendency:

- ✌ To use their ideal goal as an opening for negotiation (quite early in the negotiation)
- ✌ To be realistic with their first demands (not too high – Not too low)
- ✌ To review their bottom line goal decision during the negotiation and adjust it accordingly.

## 2. Negotiation strategy

A negotiation strategy is the answer to the question:

**How am I going to achieve my goal?**

A negotiation strategy is a planning and organizing tool. It compasses the past, present and future. It looks at the big picture and is concerned about three key negotiating issues:

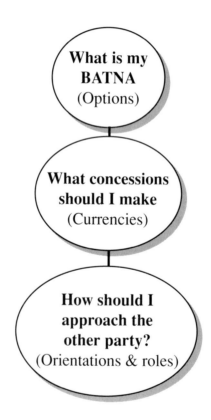

**What is my BATNA**
(Options)

**What concessions should I make**
(Currencies)

**How should I approach the other party?**
(Orientations & roles)

# What is my BATNA?

No negotiation can be effective without a good knowledge of the BATNA which has basically two meanings:

## BATNA 1

This is the **B**est **A**lternative **T**o a **N**on-**A**greement. In other words, before going to a negotiation you must identify your options. You cannot walk away from a negotiation without knowing – in advance – what your alternatives are.

## BATNA 2

This is the **B**est **A**lternative **T**o a **N**egotiated-**A**greement. The idea here is that before saying yes to a proposal, you should check your options and see if you don't have a better alternative elsewhere.

The BATNA is strategically vital in any negotiation because:

1. It helps you define and decide on your ideal objective in a realistic way.

2. It determines the level of your walk away position (the more options, the higher the bottom line, the more demanding you are going to be).

3. It gives you psychological assurance during the negotiation as well as back up solutions.

Now the negotiation model looks like this:

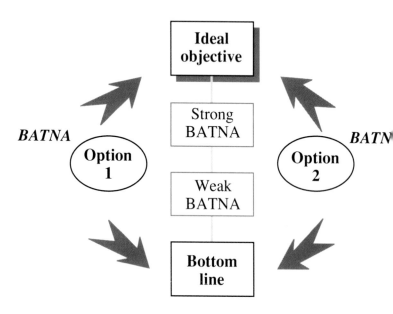

The gap between the ideal objective (maximum) and the bottom line (minimum) is established by your BATNA.

# Questions for the negotiator:

✘ Do you have a clear idea of your BATNA?

✘ Do you already know what you will do if the negotiation fails?

✘ Have you checked your options?

✘ Can you visualize the interaction between your goals (maximum – minimum) and your options? (**BATNA**)

✘ Are you implementing various concurrent negotiations? Isn't it dangerous? Is it ethical?

✘ Do you know what the other party's options (BATNA) are?

✘ Do you realize that if the other party has a strong BATNA you are going to have to be less demanding and more accommodating (and vice versa).

# Tips for the negotiator:

Good negotiators do spend some time before the negotiation to:

✌ Explore their options
*What else can I do?*

✌ Check on the other party's options
*Do they need me?*

✌ Set up their goals according to their BATNA
*How far can I go? When should I stop negotiating?*

# What concessions should I make?

A negotiator must decide – beforehand – on which concessions he or she should make and in which order. The negotiator must also look at the concessions as **currencies**.

Again the BATNA will in most cases dictate the concessions:

- ☞ **The stronger the BATNA, the fewer the concessions**
- ☞ **The weaker the BATNA, the more the concessions**

## The complete negotiation model

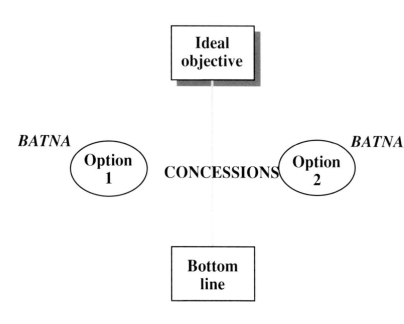

# Questions for the negotiator:

1. Have you decided on the concessions you are ready to make (nature and range)?

2. What is the **cost** of each concession?

3. How valuable are the concessions for the other party?

4. Do you have an order of priority in your concession list? What do you give away first, next… last? Why that order?

5. How do you intend to present your concessions?

6. What about the other party's currencies? What is it that he or she has that you want? Why?

# Tips for the negotiator:

**Smart negotiators:**

- Are extremely careful with their currencies. They do not give things away easily.

- Play it down when they want something from the other party and express clear "pain" when they must give something away.

- Resist the temptation to make concessions when the negotiation is close to the end.

# How should I approach the other party?

On your way to the negotiation, it is sound to review **how** you are going to conduct the negotiation (or approaches) and **who** will do what (roles) in your negotiating team (if you have one) or which roles you will play yourself (if you don't have any team).

## The orientations

Here is a brief description of three basic orientations or approaches to negotiation[1]:

## Cooperative strategy

---

1 Casse P. and Deol S.P.S., *Managing Intercultural Negotiations*. Washington D.C., SIETAR. 1985.

1. Your goal is to reach an agreement which is good and fair for everybody.

2. Win-win is your motto.

3. Trust the other party (you disclose your bottom line).

4. You are ready to compromise if necessary, but compromise should be reciprocal.

5. Appeal to common ground and joint interest.

## Comments

The cooperative strategy is certainly a powerful one – as long as the other party plays the negotiating "game" according to the same rules.

**Our advice:**

☞ Plan a cooperative strategy, **but** also have another approach ready in case the other party tries to take advantage of you.

☞ Make sure that your strategy is not perceived as a weakness by the other party.

☞ Do not disclose sensitive information too early during the negotiation.

# Competitive strategy

1. Keep in mind that if you do not get them, they will get you.

2. Be ready to fight with your cards close to your chest. Do not trust anybody.

3. Your goal is to win.

4. Demand concessions, insist on your position, apply pressure. If necessary, make threats to get what you want.

5. Give nothing. Gain everything.

## Comments

This is hard negotiation. There are times when the negotiation has to be confrontational. It cannot be otherwise. Too much is at stake to take any risk. You must be ready to fight, knowing that you cannot trust the other party, who will take advantage of you if at all possible.

**However, keep in mind:**

- You can win the battle – and lose the war?

- This type of negotiation can easily backfire, with you becoming the loser

- A competitive strategy used against a party who believes in cooperation can lead to resentment and rejection. Be careful. The negotiation you just won could cost you a lot on the side…

# Analytical strategy

1. Negotiators are problem-solvers, not fighters.

2. Negotiation should be tackled not as a "game" but as a problem-solving exercise with three main stages:

   - Stage 1    **What are the facts?** (The situation)

   - Stage 2    **What is our objective?** (Goals)

   - Stage 3    **How do we get there so that everybody is satisfied?** (Options)

3. Be creative and jointly look for alternatives.

4. Use objective criteria to make decisions.

5. Build on reason not on feelings.

# Comments

This is certainly all nice and neat, but... the real world does not always work this way. People have feelings and emotions. They are not always rational. In other words, the analytical strategy is not always applicable, especially when values and beliefs are involved in the negotiation process.

# Recommendation to the negotiator

☛ Know that all three orientations
⇨ *cooperative, competitive and analytical*, are available

☛ Learn how to use each orientation in various negotiation situations

☛ Switch to another strategy if the one you are using is not working

# The roles

It is vital that you – or your negotiating team – get your acts together before starting the negotiation.

**You must check the following:**

✗  Do you have a clear distribution of responsibilities?

✗  Are your roles well defined?

✗  Do you have a minimum of coordination?

**The roles are:**

1.  The **leader** or chief negotiator
2.  The **factual** negotiator
3.  The **analytical** negotiator
4.  The **relational** negotiator
5.  The **intuitive** negotiator

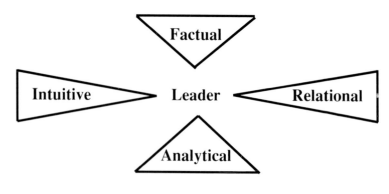

# The leader or chief negotiator

## Role description

He or she is responsible for:

1. Defining and reviewing (if necessary) the negotiation objectives, BATNA and selecting the priorities (concessions and currencies).

2. Making decisions on the content of the negotiation.

3. Making sure the strategy is implemented effectively (orientations).

4. Managing the negotiation process (tactics, roles...).

5. Reviewing the effectiveness of the negotiating team and making the required adjustment during the negotiation.

# Issues

✔ The chief negotiator is not always the person you think. For example, the hidden chief negotiator or **eminence grise** is often used in negotiations.

✔ There are formal and informal chief negotiators.

✔ It is important to check the power that you have as a chief negotiator ⇨ *how far can you go? How often will you use your power to force an issue? Isn't it to your advantage to use the head office as a power shadow during the negotiation?*

# The factual negotiator

## Role description

Factual negotiators are good at:

1. Knowing the facts related to the negotiations at hand.

2. Documenting statements.

3. Asking factual questions (probing and checking facts).

4. Answering questions to clarify points and provide complementary information upon request.

5. Being precise, so that no critical point is missed or remains uncovered.

# Issues

✔ Factual negotiators can, at times, be insensitive to the other party's emotional reactions and feelings.

✔ They can also get lost in the details of the negotiation.

✔ They eventually argue **against** team members who are not accurate in their statements, potentially weakening their side's position.

# The analytical negotiator

## Role description

Analytical negotiators are in charge of:

1. Presenting negotiating arguments in a logical way.

2. Making sure that strategy is correctly implemented, and adapted if necessary.

3. Negotiating the agenda of the meeting.

4. Establishing the rules of the negotiation.

5. Asking questions of the other party to clarify the rationale of their position, see its impact on their own negotiating team and prepare eventual adaptations to their approach.

71

# Issues

✔ Analytical negotiators can sometimes lose perspective and get too involved in arguments and counter-arguments.

✔ They are very often perceived as unemotional, cold and without feelings.

✔ Logic is not always the answer in a negotiation.

# The relational negotiator

## Role description

Relational negotiators are strong on:

1.  Facilitating relations among their negotiating team's members.
2.  Establishing and maintaining good relations with at least some members of the other team.
3.  Being sensitive to the reactions of the negotiators (importance of feelings and emotions).
4.  Building trust.
5.  Seeing the strengths and weaknesses of the opponent.

# Issues

- ✔ Relational negotiators are sometimes so involved in the human side of the negotiation that they lose track of the negotiating objectives and strategy.

- ✔ They can give away vital information without being aware of what they are doing.

- ✔ They can be highly emotional and lose perspective.

# The intuitive negotiator

## Role description

Intuitive negotiators have a knack for:

1. Coming up with ideas, new ways to approach the negotiation, potential options, etc.

2. Pinpointing what is essential in a negotiation and sorting out the key issues from the details.

3. Looking at the future implications of any proposal.

4. Pulling the pieces together and comprehending the overall negotiation or "big picture".

5. Guessing (using hunches) about the way the negotiation is going to unfold (listening to the **vibrations**).

# Issues

✔ Intuitive negotiators can be unrealistic and "danger-ous" (they sometimes have wild ideas).

✔ They do not see the shortcomings of their ideas and the risk involved in some of their proposals.

✔ They are hard to control; discipline is simply not one of their strengths.

## 3. The negotiation process

Before reaching your destination, you must know that any negotiation is contingent on some laws related to group dynamics.

Research has identified six chronological stages that any negotiation goes through:

### The six stages of a negotiation

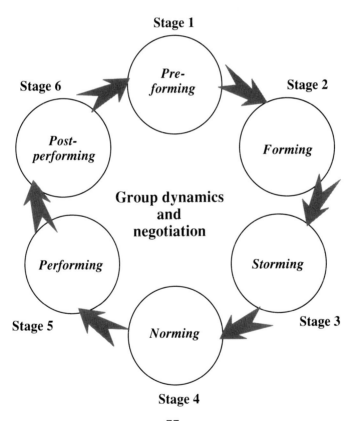

Have a look at the following description of the six stages of a negotiation and see if it fits with your own experience.

| Group Dynamics | Negotiation Stages |
|---|---|
| **1. Pre-forming** | **1. Preparation for negotiation** *Gathering negotiation intelligence* |
| • People are selected | • Negotiators are chosen and prepare themselves |
| • They get ready | • They work on their goals and strategy (as well as the other party's) |
| • They imagine things about the encounter | • They develop pre-conceived ideas about the negotiation. |

**Tips:**

✌ Watch out and control your pre-conceived ideas about the negotiation. They can handicap you during the negotiation. Remain open-minded.

✌ Prepare and… remain flexible.

✌ The more you know about them, the better off you are.

| Group Dynamics | Negotiation Stages |
|---|---|
| **2. Forming** | **2. First contact/First impression**<br>*Fact finding.* |
| • People meet for the first time | • Negotiators have their first direct contact: they assess each other! |
| • They get acquainted | • They try to get as much information as possible from the other party |
| • They try to understand who is who. | • They talk about the negotiation process (how are we going to proceed?) |

**Tips:**

✌ Keep in mind that the first impression is always critical (control and manage it).

✌ Always prepare thoroughly your **first statement**. Do not improvise. It will set up the negotiating tone in most cases.

✌. Use your **factual** behaviour as much as possible.

| Group Dynamics | Negotiation Stages |
|---|---|
| **3. Storming** | **3. Confrontation stage**<br>*Argumenting* |
| • Opinions are expressed | • Differences in expectations are progressively pointed out |
| • Differences in perceptions and appreciations (judgments) are identified | • Arguments are vividly presented and exchanged |
| • Oppositions surface (power issues) | • Some heat develops... trust is the issue... negotiators are anxious to know who is going to win. |

**Tips:**

✌ It is now time to "package" your arguments and sell your ideas **matching** the negotiating style(s) of the other party.

✌ Be **analytical**.

✌ Control your emotions and feelings. Do not get carried away.

80

| Group Dynamics | Negotiation Stages |
|---|---|
| **4. Norming** | **4. Conciliation stage**<br>*Bargaining* |
| • The group tries to set up rules to function effectively | • Use of **compromises.** (I give away something and you do the same… and we are then OK) |
| • Power is distributed and individual identities recognized | • Use of **synthesis**. (Let's see if we can accommodate your position and mine as well) |
| • People get organized. They have developed a group culture with a set of common:<br>- values<br>- normsl<br>- behavioural patterns | • Use of **synergy**. (Can we come up with new options, new ways to solve our problem?) |

**Tips:**

❦ It is time to use the **"if… then"** negotiating behaviour.

❦ Be creative. There is always a solution to any problem. Be **intuitive**.

❦ Keep in mind that a concession justifies a concession in return.

| Group Dynamics | Negotiation Stages |
|---|---|
| **5. Performing** | **3. Solution stage**<br>*Agreeing* |
| • It is the implementation phase. Now the group members are able to work together effectively. | • Through **give and take**, the negotiators find their way around. |
| • Results are achieved and feedback given to the group. | • They know where they stand and negotiate the real issues. They do it step by step. One success leads to another. They feel they are getting somewhere. |
| • The group reviews its own performance and makes the necessary adjustments. | • They agree and… feel uncomfortable wondering if they have made the right decision, or if they have been **had**. |

**Tips:**

&#9977;    Identify common grounds and build on agreements.

&#9977;    Summarize from time to time and check your understandings.

&#9977;    Develop good shared feelings. Be **relational**. ("We have both won!")

| Group Dynamics | Negotiation Stages |
|---|---|
| **6. Post-performing** | **6. Post-negotiation** |
| • People leave and experience a down (separation) | • Now is the real test: *"Did we really agree? Are we committed? How do we feel?"* |
| • They feel sad and disoriented | • Some follow-up is required to make sure that the implementation is right |
| • The decisions made by the group are now implemented | • Contacts should be maintained with the other party (on-going negotiation). |

**Tips:**

✌ Do not believe that the negotiation has ended. This is now the most difficult point: **to translate the agreements into action**.

✌ Build on your success. Network. Be **relational**.

✌ Consolidate and learn from the experience. Improve your negotiating knowledge and skills.

# Reviewing the planning steps of a negotiation

Without looking at the previous pages, try to summarize the key success factors (what you must do to be an effective negotiator) related to:

1.  **The negotiation goals:**

    ...............................................................................

    ...............................................................................

    ...............................................................................

2.  **The negotiation strategy:**

    ...............................................................................

    ...............................................................................

    ...............................................................................

3.  **The negotiation process:**

    ...............................................................................

    ...............................................................................

    ...............................................................................

# The negotiation planning step

## *Summary*

1.  Enhance your ability to negotiate in **competing, cooperative** and **analytical** modes. The more modes you are competent with, the more flexible you can be… and the greater your chances for success.

2.  Five roles are indispensable when you negotiate:

    - ✔ **Leader**
    - ✔ **Factual**
    - ✔ **Analytical**
    - ✔ **Relational**
    - ✔ **Intuitive**

    Which one(s) can you play? Where are you strong? Weak? What about your negotiating team?

3.  Your **N**egotiating **A**ction **P**lan (NAP) should take the six following negotiation stages into account:

    - ✔ **Preparation**
    - ✔ **First contact** (first impressions)
    - ✔ **Confrontation**
    - ✔ **Conciliation**
    - ✔ **Solution**
    - ✔ **Consolidation**

    You must determine who will do what, when and how, before going to negotiation.

## Nice ideas…

## but how do we implement them?

# CHAPTER 4

## The negotiation implementation step

# *During*

**Implementing** is the translation of ideas into action or behaviour. It is **doing**. Not primarily thinking anymore, but rather achieving.

Negotiation implementation has the following key components:

- **Negotiating tactics**
- **Negotiating skills**
- **Negotiating behaviours**

Let's review them one by one.

# Negotiation tactics

A tactic is part of an implementation strategy. It is a set of manoeuvres executed in a logical manner so that some short term, limited objectives are achieved. Tactics are what negotiators do when involved in the bargaining situation. They are related to the "here and now" of the negotiation.

Let's examine four well known negotiation tactics:

**1.** Going our way

**2.** Going along

**3.** Going nowhere

**4.** Going
somewhere else

# Tactic 1

## *Going our way*

This tactic is characterized by the following features:

- ✔ We know where we want to go.
- ✔ We argue and **push** to convince the other party that we are right.
- ✔ We take the initiative and hold it.
- ✔ We control the negotiating process.
- ✔ We keep pressing.

You will recognize this tactic when somebody:

- ✌ Takes the lead.
- ✌ Actively looks for options and solutions.
- ✌ Explains his ideas, demonstrates, argues in favour of his proposal, defines what he means, appeals, attacks…

This tactic (which is sometimes identified as **pushing** or **moving against**) can be used in a subtle way ("Nice and easy"), in an aggressive way ("Give them hell") or with a mixture of subtlety and aggression ("Hot and cold water alternately").

# Tactic 2

## *Going along*

Going along implies

- ✔ We want to listen to the other party and see what he has in mind.
- ✔ We have decided to be reactive (not pro-active).
- ✔ We are ready to go along if what he proposes is in line with our objectives.
- ✔ We agree, disagree and sometimes build upon their ideas. We are constructive when it is to our advantage.
- ✔ We make them work.

You will recognize this tactic when somebody:

- ✌ Plays the role of a follower.
- ✌ Asks for more information.
- ✌ Probes your ideas.
- ✌ Disagrees, without providing any alternative.
- ✌ Listens a lot and asks numerous questions.

Here again, the tactic can be used in a positive and constructive way ("I trust you"), in a very hard mode ("I do not trust your statements") or with a mixture of both.

# Tactic 3

## *Going nowhere*

Going nowhere is to play stubborn. We do not move. We want to stay where we are (at least for the time being). We resist any idea to change anything. We play deadlock.

We do this because:

- ✔ We want to think about something.
- ✔ We are interested in gaining time.
- ✔ We are trying to make the other party nervous. Time is in our favour.
- ✔ We believe it is time to take stock, put things into perspective…

# Tactic 4

## *Going somewhere else*

Here we are extremely active because we have decided to avoid the issue, to go around it, not to talk about it (at least now) and switch to another topic because:

- ✔ We are convinced that it is to our advantage to skip the issue for the time being.

- ✔ It will make the issue more important in the other party's eyes.

- ✔ The time is not right.

- ✔ Another agreement should be made first.

Some other common negotiation tactics can also be listed. Do you know them? Have you used them?

| Tactics | Advantages | Disadvantages |
|---|---|---|
| **1.** Delaying on purpose | Time is in our favour. We are not ready yet | Risk of a deadlock at the end of the negotiation. |
| **2.** Salami (one request at a time) | Do not scare the other party, obtain small concessions, difficulty to say no at the end of the negotiation | Create mistrust |
| **3.** Ultimatum or the use of threats in negotiation ("Take it or leave it") | Force the issue | The negotiation can stop all together |
| **4.** Last minute demand | Take the other party by surprise | Can jeopardize the entire negotiation process and what has been achieved so far |
| **5.** If... then... | No commitment. It is just a hypothesis. Probing and exploring possibilities. | Reinforce the bargaining mood of the negotiation. |

97

# Negotiation skills

Here, now, are the skills you need to be an effective negotiator. They are presented in two sets:

- ✔ Conventional skills for conventional negotiators

- ✔ Unconventional skills for unconventional negotiators

## Question

Are you a **conventional** or **unconventional** negotiator?

Look at the **skills** and decide for yourself:

# Conventional negotiating skills[1]

| Definition | Advantages | Disadvantages |
|---|---|---|
| 1. Using **open-ended questions** – questions that cannot be answered by a yes or no (They start with what, who, when, why…). | Extremely effective for gathering information from the other party, clarifying positions and channelling the discussion. | Can be perceived as a threat by the other negotiator (especially any question starting with "**why**"?). |
| 2. **Paraphrasing** or re-formulating (feeding back) what the other negotiator said, using your own words. (*"If I understand correctly, you said…"*). | Enables you to:<br>• show interest<br>• check your understanding of what the other party said<br>• gain time to prepare your answer<br>• give an opportunity to the opponent to add something. | Can slow down the negotiation process and give the sense you are not actively involved. Can trigger some frustration. |
| 3. Using **silence** either after a question or right after a statement made by the other party. (If you do not talk, there is a good chance s/he will start again…). | Extremely well used by Asian negotiators. Forces the other party to share more information with you (unplanned disclosure). | Can be seen as offensive, triggering negative reactions as well as anxiety. |
| 4. **Summarizing** from time to time to keep track of the key points covered during the negotiation. | Can be used at various checkpoints to measure progress of the negotiation and build upon previous agreements. | It forces you to go back to some points that you do not necessarily want to cover again. |
| 5. **Acknowledging feelings and emotions** to ease tension and reinforce trust. | Deals with the human dimension of the negotiation, which can never be underestimated. | You know where it starts, but you never know where it will end. (Negotiation is not a psychotherapy exercise). |

---

[1] Take one minute during your negotiations to glance at this sheet to refresh your mind about these skills, their advantages and disadvantages.

99

# Unconventional negotiating skills[1]

| Definition | Advantages | Disadvantages |
|---|---|---|
| 1. **Misunderstanding** the other party on purpose through a mistaken reformulation, question or summary. | The other negotiator is "forced" to clarify his or her position and add some information. | Can lead to ambiguity and frustration. |
| 2. **Exaggerating** through the amplification of what the other negotiator says. Using words like "always", "never", "impossible", "nobody", "everybody", "extremely"... | Extremely good in order to preempt an extreme position that you know the other party is ready to take ("*I know you believe this is impossible...*"). | Used without subtlety, the skill can be seen as pure manipulation, and create a deadlock. |
| 3. **Unexpected move.** You say or do something not in line with what is being discussed. You switch to something else, unexpectedly. | Creates a surprise effect that you can eventually take advantage of... The other negotiator tries to understand what you are after... He has lost the "logic" of the argument. | Dangerous. It works **once**... and it can lead to rejection and aggressiveness. |
| 4. Being **sarcastic.** Using mockery at the expense of the other negotiator.. | Can provoke emotional reactions, as well as assertive behaviour. ("*Is it what you want?*") | The other party can just walk out on you... |
| 5. **Overloading** the other party with a lot of questions, or too much information. | The negotiator must understand, weigh and decide on how to use this information. He is in a weak position. You can either help, or... | Success with this skill depends on the capacity of the other party to absorb information. Can lead to mistrust. |

---

[1] Take one minute during your negotiations to glance at this sheet to review these skills if you use them at all – or if you use them properly.

# Negotiation behaviours

Here are five checklists presenting what the successful negotiator's behaviours are according to:

- ✔ The Huthwaite Research Group
- ✔ Casse and Deol
- ✔ Nierenberg
- ✔ Fisher and Ury
- ✔ Bellenger

We suggest that you use each checklist as a **self-assessment exercise** to measure your ability or inability to use the described behaviours.

## Now, let's see how you do...

# The findings of the Huthwaite Research Group[1]

**When you negotiate, are you able to:**

|  |  | Yes | Not always | No |
|---|---|:---:|:---:|:---:|
| **1.** | Consider a high number of alternatives per issue… | ☐ | ☐ | ☐ |
| **2.** | Look for areas of common ground… | ☐ | ☐ | ☐ |
| **3.** | Focus on long term implications rather than short term… | ☐ | ☐ | ☐ |
| **4.** | Take up issues independent of one another… | ☐ | ☐ | ☐ |
| **5.** | Avoid words and remarks which irritate the other party… | ☐ | ☐ | ☐ |

**Questions:**   **1.** What do you have to be careful with?

.......................................................................

.......................................................................

**2.** How can you improve?

.......................................................................

.......................................................................

---

[1] Huthwaite Research Group. *The Behavior of Successful Negotiators.* 1976, Reston, Va.

102

# The Casse-Deol pointers[1]

**When you negotiate, are you able to:**

|  |  | Yes | Not always | No |
|---|---|---|---|---|
| **1.** | Help the other party expand on his ideas… | ❏ | ❏ | ❏ |
| **2.** | Probe an idea in a neutral manner… | ❏ | ❏ | ❏ |
| **3.** | Express support for an idea presented by the other party… | ❏ | ❏ | ❏ |
| **4.** | Disagree in a constructive way… | ❏ | ❏ | ❏ |
| **5.** | Assess the values of your own and the other party's idea… | ❏ | ❏ | ❏ |

**Questions:**  **1.** What is your major weakness?

.........................................................................

.........................................................................

**2.** How are you going to change?

.........................................................................

.........................................................................

---

[1]  Casse, P., and Deol, S.P.S. *Managing Intercultural Negotiation*. Washington: SIETAR, 1985.

# The Nierenberg recommendations[1]

**When you negotiate, are you able to:**

|  |  | Yes | Not always | No |
|---|---|---|---|---|
| **1.** | Get and give information in a controlled way... | ❑ | ❑ | ❑ |
| **2.** | Make others think | ❑ | ❑ | ❑ |
| **3.** | Leave the other party with the assumption that s/he has been answered... | ❑ | ❑ | ❑ |
| **4.** | Bring others' thinking to a conclusion... | ❑ | ❑ | ❑ |
| **5.** | Leave the other party with the desire to pursue the questioning process further... | ❑ | ❑ | ❑ |

**Questions:**  **1.** What is your major strength?

..................................................................

..................................................................

**2.** How can you build on your strength?

..................................................................

..................................................................

---

[1] Nierenberg, G.I. *Creative Business Negotiation.* N.Y.: Hawthorne Books, 1971.

# The Fisher and Ury checklist[1]

**When you negotiate, are you able to:**

|   |   | Yes | Not always | No |
|---|---|---|---|---|
| **1.** | Separate the people from the problem… | ❐ | ❐ | ❐ |
| **2.** | Focus on interests, not positions… | ❐ | ❐ | ❐ |
| **3.** | Come up with options for mutual gain… | ❐ | ❐ | ❐ |
| **4.** | Invite criticism and advice… | ❐ | ❐ | ❐ |
| **5.** | Avoid the vicious cycle of attack and counterattack… | ❐ | ❐ | ❐ |

**Questions:**   **1.** Where do you have difficulty?

..............................................................

..............................................................

**2.** Why?

..............................................................

..............................................................

---

[1] Fisher, R., and Ury, W. *Getting to Yes*. Penguin Books, 1984.

# The Bellenger model[1]

**When you negotiate, are you able to:**

|  | | Yes | Not always | No |
|---|---|---|---|---|
| **1.** | Analyse the facts to determine what the parties' positions are… | ❐ | ❐ | ❐ |
| **2.** | Get issues out in the open… | ❐ | ❐ | ❐ |
| **3.** | Argue toward reducing gaps between the parties' positions… | ❐ | ❐ | ❐ |
| **4.** | Pinpoint areas of agreement and disagreement… | ❐ | ❐ | ❐ |
| **5.** | Compromise… | ❐ | ❐ | ❐ |

**Questions:**   **1.** What kind of a negotiator would you like to be?

...................................................................

...................................................................

**2.** How do you intend to become more effective?

...................................................................

...................................................................

---

[1] Bellenger, L. *Les techniques d'argumentation et de négociation.* Paris: EME, 1978.

# Take one minute to check on your negotiating profile:

| Negotiation | Strengths _What I do well_ | Weaknesses _What I don't do well_ |
|---|---|---|
| **1. Tactics** | 1. ............................ <br><br> 2. ............................ <br><br> 3. ............................ | 1. ............................ <br><br> 2. ............................ <br><br> 3. ............................ |
| **2. Skills** | 1. ............................ <br><br> 2. ............................ <br><br> 3. ............................ | 1. ............................ <br><br> 2. ............................ <br><br> 3. ............................ |
| **3. Behaviours** | 1. ............................ <br><br> 2. ............................ <br><br> 3. ............................ | 1. ............................ <br><br> 2. ............................ <br><br> 3. ............................ |

## Work now on how to improve your negotiating behaviour:

| What I should stop doing | What I should do differently | What I should start doing |
|---|---|---|
| 1. ............................. ............................. ............................. | 1. ............................. ............................. ............................. | 1. ............................. ............................. ............................. |
| 2. ............................. ............................. ............................. | 2. ............................. ............................. ............................. | 2. ............................. ............................. ............................. |
| 3. ............................. ............................. ............................. | 3. ............................. ............................. ............................. | 3. ............................. ............................. ............................. |

# The implementation step in negotiating:

## *Summary*

1. Effective negotiators know how to push, pull, avoid and do nothing. They master a range of negotiation **tactics**.

2. They are able to use **conventional negotiation skills** (can you name the five listed in this part of the book?) as well as **unconventional** ones (what are they?) according to the requirements of the bargaining situation they find themselves in.

3. Successful negotiators are distinguished by these behaviours:

   - They know what they want. *"At the end of the negotiation, I'll be happy if..."*

   - When they do not get what they want, they do not just reemphasize or amplify what they are already doing. Rather, **they switch to something else!** *"Let me try something else".*

   - They know when they have what they want, and they never leave the negotiation without consolidating its outcome. *"Let's agree on what we have agreed upon".*

**…and where do we go from here?**

# CHAPTER 5

## The negotiation review step

# *After*

Reviewing is critical in any negotiation because it enables you to:

✗ Check whether you have achieved your objective.
*Did I get what I wanted?*

✗ If not, examine what went wrong and learn from the experience.
*What can I do to avoid the same mistakes in the future?*

✗ If yes, determine what you did right and build on your success.
*Can I repeat that later on?*

**"Learning how to learn"** is the key to success for all negotiators. That implies:

### Learning how to learn when negotiating[1]

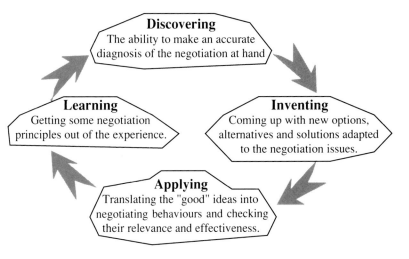

---

[1] Casse, P., *Training for the Cross-Cultural Mind*. Washington: SIETAR, 1986.

There are basically three kinds of review:

1. During the negotiation (monitoring) – in order to:
   ✗ See how you are doing
   ✗ Spot what's good and bad for you in the ongoing negotiation
   ✗ Adjust (if necessary and possible) your objectives, strategies and tactics

2. Right after the negotiation (post-review) – in order to:
   ✗ Think about the implementation of the agreement and prepare for potential problems
   ✗ Assess your negotiation effectiveness
   ✗ Decide on key areas for improvement

3. Sometime after the negotiation (post-evaluation) – in order to:
   ✗ Assess your review process
   ✗ Check on the implementation of the agreement
   ✗ Verify your growth as a negotiator.

# A simplified checklist on reviewing the negotiation process:

**What:** The main purpose of the review is to compare what has been achieved to what had been planned (outputs versus expectations). It is done in relation to:

- Goals

- Strategy

- Tactics

**How:** The review process can be informal or formal. It is generally organized both ways. It is recommended to have somebody in the negotiating team taking notes so that the review is more accurate and effective. The review can take place:

- During the breaks (informal)

- At the end of the day, the week... (formal)

**When:** On an ongoing basis – and, especially, **when it is needed**. You can have emergency reviews (when there is a crisis) and also pre-planned reviews (at designated checkpoints).

**Who:** The chief negotiator is generally responsible for making sure that the reviews take place when necessary and scheduled.

**Why:** To check on results and decide on improvements.

Let's face it – reviewing is the weakest spot of many negotiators.

They get so involved in the act of negotiating that they forget to stop, take stock, put things into perspective and... **improve.**

**Take one minute to review your ability
to do these things**

# The negotiation review action list

Assuming you are on your way to a negotiation:

|  |  | Yes | No |
|---|---|---|---|
| **1.** | Have you decided on your review checkpoints... | ☐ | ☐ |
| **2.** | Have you explained to your team members why and when you will review the negotiation process... | ☐ | ☐ |
| **3.** | Have you appointed somebody in the team who will keep track of the main events of the negotiation... | ☐ | ☐ |
| **4.** | Do you have a "review checklist" handy... | ☐ | ☐ |
| **5.** | Do you have a list of criteria you will use to decide if the negotiation is going well or not... | ☐ | ☐ |

**If you have marked "no" five times... You are in trouble!**

Review the life case hereunder and identify:

1.  The three key negotiations involved in the case

2.  The three major negotiating problems that the CEO must cope with

3.  Three things the CEO should do to improve.

# The case of the frustrated engineer[1]

## Background

The organisation in question is a venture that was started in the early 70s. While working for one of the fairly innovative electronics firms, a group of engineers developed a new electronics product. However, they were in a division that did not have the charter for their product. The ensuing political battle caused the engineers to **leave** and form their own company. They successfully found venture capital and introduced their new product. Initial acceptance was good, and within several years their company was growing rapidly and had become the industry leader.

However, in the early 1970s Intel invented the microprocessor, and by the mid- to late 70s, this innovation had spread through the electronics industries. Manufacturers of previously "dumb" products now had the capability of incorporating intelligence into their product lines. A competitor who understood computers and softwares introduced just such a product into the new venture firm's market, and it met with high

---

[1] Galbraith J.R.in *Organization*, J.P. Kotter, L.A. Schlesinger, V. Sathe.1986, Irwin, Homewood, IL. Adapted by P. Casse.

acceptance. The firm's president responded by hiring someone who knew something about microcomputers and some software people and instructing the engineering department to respond to the need for a competing product.

The president spent most of his time raising capital to finance the venture's growth. But when he suddenly realized that the engineers had not made much progress, he instructed them to get a product out quickly. They did, but it was a half-hearted effort. The new product incorporated a microprocessor but was less than the second-generation product that was called for.

## The deadlock

Even though the president developed markets in Europe and Singapore, he noticed that the competitor continued to grow faster than his company and had started to steal a share of his company's market. When the competitor became the industry leader, the president decided to take charge of the product development effort. However, he found that the hardware proponents and software proponents in the engineering department were locked in a political battle. Each group felt that its "magic" was the more powerful. Unfortunately, the lead engineer (who was a co-founder of the firm) was a hardware proponent, and the hardware establishment prevailed. However, they then clashed head-on with the marketing department, which agreed with the software proponents. The conflict resulted in studies and presentations, but no new product. So here was a young, small (1,200 people) entrepreneurial firm that could not innovate though the president wanted innovation and provided resources to produce it. The lesson is that more was needed.

## Seeing the light

As the president became more and more deeply involved in the problem, he received a call from his New England sales manager, who wanted him to meet a field manager who had modified the company's product and programmed it in a way that met customer demands. The sales manager suggested: "We may have something here".

Indeed, the president was impressed with what he saw. When the engineer had wanted to use the company's product to track his own inventory, he wrote to company headquarters for programming instructions. The response had been: "It's against company policy to send instructional materials to field engineers". Undaunted, the engineer bought a home computer and taught himself to program. He then modified the product in the field and programmed it to solve his problem. When the sales manager happened to see what was done, he recognized its significance and immediately called the president.

The field engineer accompanied the president back to headquarters and presented his work to the engineers who had been working on the second-generation product for so long. They brushed off his efforts as idiosyncratic, and the field engineer was thanked and returned to the field.

## Success and frustration

A couple of weeks later the sales manager called the president again. He said that the company would lose this talented guy if something wasn't done. Besides, he thought that the field engineer, not engineering, was right. While he was considering what to do with this ingenious engineer who on his own had produced more than the entire engineering department, the president received a request from the European sales manager to have the engineer assigned to him.

The European sales manager had heard about the field engineer when he visited headquarters, and had sought him out and listened to his story. The sales manager knew that a French bank wanted the type of application that the field engineer had created for himself; a successful application would be worth an order for several hundred machines. The president gave the go-ahead and sent the field engineer to Europe. The engineering department persisted in their view that the program wouldn't work. Three months later, the field engineer successfully developed the application, and the bank signed the order.

When the field engineer returned, the president assigned him to a trusted marketing manager who was told to protect him and get a product out. The engineers were told to support the manager and reluctantly did so. Soon they created some applications software and a printed circuit board that could easily be installed in all existing machines in the field. The addition of this board and the software temporarily saved the company and made its current product slightly superior to that of the competitor.

## What next?

Elated, the president congratulated the young field engineer and gave him a good staff position working on special assignments to develop software. Then problems arose. When the president tried to get the personnel department to give the engineer a special cash award, they were reluctant. "After all", they said, "other people worked on the effort, too. It will set a precedent". And so it went. The finance department wanted to withold $500 from the engineer's pay because he had received a $1,000 advance for his European trip, but had turned in vouchers for only $500.

The engineer didn't help himself very much either; he was hard to get along with and refused to accept supervision from anyone except the European sales manager. When the president arranged to have him permanently transferred to Europe on three occasions, the engineer changed his mind about going at the last minute. The president is still wondering what to do with him.

# Debriefing

1.  The three key negotiations are:

    1.  Negotiation between the engineers and the marketing specialists

    2.  Negotiation between the CEO and the field engineer

    3.  Negotiation between the engineering department and the field engineer.

2.  The three major negotiating problems:

    1.  Keeping the field engineer on board

    2.  Change the engineering department and make it more innovative

    3.  Improve the relationship between the head office and the field.

3.  Three things the CEO should do:

    1.  Stop running around and start leading the company

    2.  Learn how to lead innovative people (entrepreneurs) and integrate their work into the mainstream of the company

    3.  Set up a new incentive system to reward good performance.

# The negotiation review step

## *Summary*

Taking stock during the negotiation is essential in order to:

- Measure your effectiveness. *"Is it working?"*
- Decide on adjustments. *"Should I modify my attitudes, behaviours, orientations, roles..."*
- Check on your negotiation plan. *"Are my goals still valid? What about my concessions and currencies?..."*

The after-negotiation review is also vital so that you can learn from what you just did, build on your strengths and control your weaknesses. *"What have I learned from my last negotiation?"*.

# CHAPTER 6

**Learning from shrewd negotiators**

To have the knowledge is not enough. You must be able to do the right thing, the right way, at the right time.

Let's watch the seasoned negotiators and see what they do...

Watch the old timers – the powerful, successful negotiators – and learn from their:

## Attitudes

and

## Behaviours

Before proceeding, one word of caution. In negotiation, it is always useful to remember that:

- ✌ What's good for one person is not necessarily good for another. We are all different.

- ✌ What's effective in one situation is not automatically effective in another situation. Situational requirements change.

- ✌ What's relevant today can be obsolete tomorrow. Time is a factor that must be considered.

# The successful negotiator's attitudes

It seems that experienced negotiators are very much aware of, and sensitive to:

✔ **Time** and its impact on the unfolding of the negotiation. Is there too much or too little time? Is it too early or too late for certain aspects of the negotiation?

Expert negotiators are extremely good at "managing" time to their advantage:

- Slowing down or... speeding up (switching gears).

- Allocating time to different agenda items.

- Breaking sessions at the right moment, for the right duration.

- Pressing the other party – when the time is ripe.

- Using deadlines effectively.

✔ The **environment** and its various components, i.e.:

- Where people sit (who faces whom).

- The kind of table or setting.

- The lights, space, decoration of the room, the windows...

Veteran, successful negotiators are extremely careful with the physical environment of the negotiation, without mentioning the choice of the location (neutral, my place, your place...). They always want to have a look at the room in which the negotiation will take place prior to the opening session.

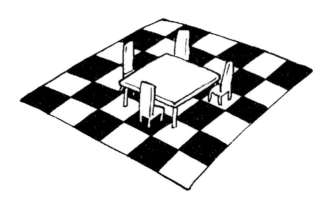

✔ The **protocol** of the negotiation, or how the negotiation is going to be conducted – i.e.:

- How many people will participate.

- Titles of the negotiating partners.

- Power and authority.

- Agenda.

- Rules regarding who speaks first, last, facilitates, leads, presence or absence of a chairman...

Observing them in action, you will notice that excellent negotiators believe the first solution to a negotiation dilemma is seldom the best one; they never, ever take "no" for an answer; they are convinced that there is always a way around a deadlock; and they trust their intuition. They listen, carefully, to the vibrations...

They also care about:

✌ The way they dress.

✌ The jewellery they wear.

✌ The documents they bring to the negotiation.

**And even more important...**

✔ The **silent language** used during the negotiation:

1. **The eyes:** where do you look? How do you look? For how long do you look?...

2. **The facial expressions:** showing concern, amusement, happiness, anger, disagreement, agreement, showing the teeth...

3. **The voice:** tone, pitch, speed of delivery...

4. **The gestures:** impatient, offering, pushing back...

5. **The foot:** tapping, locked into the chair...

6. **The body posture:** sitting comfortably, leaning forward, backward...

7. **The hand:** open, closed...

8. **The distance:** far away, very close, touching...

## The secret weapons of shrewd negotiators

Here are five negotiating behaviours you should be careful with. When you see them, watch out – a shrewd negotiator is using them on you! When you use them yourself, do it with proper care, because they are indeed powerful and can backfire when misused.

# Secret weapon No 1

When you hear a negotiator say, *"Oh! That reminds me of a story..."* –
**be alert – at once.** Watch your step and listen carefully to the other party
because he or she is using (consciously or not) a negotiating weapon on
you.

A **story** is always dangerous in the sense that it is a **metaphor** and has
at least two meanings:

✔   The overt meaning – the story itself, but also

✔   The covert meaning, which is the message within the
    message that is directed towards your unconscious
    mind rather than your consciousness.

In other words, you are being targeted for a message that you are not
aware of! This could be highly manipulative...

**Recommendation:**   Use **metaphors** when you negotiate.

# Secret weapon No 2

Some negotiators are extremely skilful at playing a "game" on other people. They put you in a frame which, if accepted, limits considerably your options as well as your freedom to manoeuvre.

That is what we call:   **The false option approach,** or
                        **the illusion of choice**

For instance they will say:

✘   Do you prefer to discuss this now, or tomorrow morning?
    *How about tonight, or in a week, or maybe never?*

✘   Do you want to start with a discussion on the overall agenda or on negotiating procedures?
    *How about the timing of the negotiation, the choice of the negotiators…?*

With this weapon, the negotiator in front of you wants to make sure that you do not consider some other things. What are they? Why does he want to avoid them? These are questions you should ask yourself.

**Recommendation:**   **Frame** the negotiation to your advantage.

# Secret weapon No 3

Have you ever heard a negotiator say (generally with a nice, soft voice), *"Let's see where we are. We met at 08:30 this morning, we first talked about our agenda, we then spent two hours on the first items of the agenda, you expressed some concern about our proposal; we presented a new option, you reacted favourably, we moved on until 10:30 and had a break..."*.

Everything is fine here... except that **one item** is not right. *"You reacted favourably"*. The problem is that you started to check everything he said at the beginning. After a while, you stopped checking – and that is precisely when he sandwiched in that misstatement. That's what we call **smooth transitions.**

**Recommendation:**  Use **smooth transitions** to check out the other party

# Secret weapon No 4

Our advice is that you should always look for expressions like:

**"It has been shown…"**      **"Specialists have discovered…"**
**"Experts say…"**      **"Researchers have found…"**

Each time that a negotiator uses one of those, he or she is simply playing a trick on you – selling his ideas with a big screen or cover.

If this is done in a subtle way, there is a good chance that you will be intimidated. You will hesitate to reject the idea, or at least hesitate to argue with all the strength that you should.

Using others to sell your ideas has a double advantage:

    ✌    You get credibility.

    ✌    Nobody can attack you personally on those ideas –
        because they are not yours.

That's what a good **screen** is all about.

**Recommendation:**    Use **screens** to sell your ideas as much as possible.

# Secret weapon No 5

Finally, think about those negotiators who say, with a nice smile on their face: *"I like what you said very much. I agree with you that we should be extremely careful and wait a bit more before signing this contract."*

Everything looks fine. Except that you never said anything about waiting. That's what the other party added to your argument. It is devious. It starts with good, positive reinforcement by paraphrasing what you said. But then the other negotiator includes a little thing that you will not notice if you are enjoying your apparent "victory" (not quite). This is **overbuilding** (or twisting) your argument. Watch out.

**Recommendation:**   Be alert and tactfully use this weapon too.

…and what do you think of these other negotiating weapons:

- ✔ The "placebo effect"…
- ✔ Using generalizations…
- ✔ Extrapolating…
- ✔ Using quotes…
- ✔ Misquoting, and then making the right correction…

You can also use these weapons when you negotiate. Just remember that only experienced negotiators are able to do this with

## elegance!

# The shrewd negotiator's attitudes and behaviours

## *Summary*

1.  Successful negotiators pay attention to:
    - Time
    - Setting
    - Protocol

    ...as negotiation factors.


2.  They also use powerful weapons that nobody talks about, such as:
    - The **story** or **metaphor** approach
    - The **illusion of choice** (Negotiation framing and reframing)
    - **Smooth** (misleading) **transitions**
    - The **screen statement**
    - **Overbuilding** or **twisting**


3.  Effectively using these weapons requires **elegance**.

# CHAPTER 7

## Difficult cases in negotiation

# Five dilemmas

Read these descriptions of negotiating dilemmas. Pick the best option from the three presented. Then check, on the following page, our thoughts on your choice.

## Dilemma 1

You have been negotiating for several days with the representatives of a company your firm is interested in merging with.

What they are asking for is unrealistic. You know they are bluffing. Do you:

**Option 1:** Confront them with their bluff?

**Option 2:** Push for a compromise, showing them in a subtle way that you are aware of the bluff?

**Option 3:** Negotiate as if you knew nothing?

**Your reactions and comments:**

✎ ....................................................................

.........................................................................

.........................................................................

.........................................................................

.........................................................................

.........................................................................

# Comments

**Option 1:**  It can be risky and lead to either deadlock or a walk-out reaction. (Watch out for the face-saving syndrome.)

**Option 2:**  Yes, that looks smart! The question is, *how do you show that you know they are bluffing?* Can you use some factual hints here and there, or speak to a member of the other team informally…

**Option 3:**  This is dangerous because they will negotiate on the premise that you know nothing. The more they go on, the deeper they will get into this fiction – and the more difficult it will be later on to have a fair, honest negotiation.

# Dilemma 2

During a negotiation, an offer is made to you which is not quite bribery, but certainly illegal. Do you:

**Option 1:** Reject it right away and break off the negotiation?

**Option 2:** Go on with the negotiation as if you had heard nothing?

**Option 3:** Tell the other party that you do not do business that way, and pursue the negotiation on a straight basis?

**Your reactions and comments:**

✎ .......................................................................................
..........................................................................................
..........................................................................................
..........................................................................................
..........................................................................................
..........................................................................................
..........................................................................................
..........................................................................................
..........................................................................................
..........................................................................................
..........................................................................................

# Comments

**Option 1:** Yes, but… can you afford it? What's at stake? Think twice before using this option.

**Option 2:** Well… it depends on the situation. In most cases, it will be difficult for you to ignore the "offer". Besides, to say nothing could be interpreted as an agreement…

**Option 3:** This looks like the best way to handle this delicate situation, as long as it is done in a tactful and diplomatic manner.

# Dilemma 3

You are the chief negotiator for a team involved in a business negotiation over a big contract with the government. In the middle of a session, one of your team members took a misguided initiative which went against your planned strategy. Do you:

**Option 1:** Ask for a break and have a talk with your colleague?

**Option 2:** Take the floor and make sure he is not going to talk anymore?

**Option 3:** Tell him he is wrong in a nice but firm way, and go on with the negotiation?

**Your reactions and comments:**

✎ ..............................................................................

..............................................................................

..............................................................................

..............................................................................

..............................................................................

..............................................................................

..............................................................................

..............................................................................

..............................................................................

..............................................................................

..............................................................................

# Comments

**Option 1:** This is certainly a nice way to deal with the problem. The hitch is, *what are you going to do to make the necessary correction*, without showing internal disagreement?

**Option 2:** Very good, but… do not believe that the other party is not going to notice anything. The question remains, *how do you make the needed correction?*

**Option 3:** Risky, but maybe right. Everything depends on the seriousness of the deviation and the reaction of your team member. One advantage is that the other party will get the message regarding your formal position and who is in charge!

# Dilemma 4

Deeply involved in a negotiation, and taking advantage of a good reaction from the other party, you have agreed to something beyond your mandate. You know that there is a high risk that headquarters (your boss) will not approve your decision. Do you:

**Option 1:** Go ahead, hoping that success will speak for itself?

**Option 2:** Withdraw, telling the other party that you must get final approval on this point from headquarters?

**Option 3:** Say nothing to the other party, and call headquarters during a break?

**Your reactions and comments:**

✎ ...............................................................................

...................................................................................

...................................................................................

...................................................................................

...................................................................................

...................................................................................

...................................................................................

...................................................................................

...................................................................................

...................................................................................

# Comments

**Option 1:** Good luck. What if headquarters does not approve your decision? Could mean big trouble. Can you afford it?

**Option 2:** Safe, but… There is a possibility that you will lose some of your credibility, at least in the eyes of the other party.

**Option 3:** Good enough. What do you do if headquarters says no?

# Dilemma 5

The chief representative of the union has just told you that if his proposal has not been approved by midnight, the entire workforce will go on strike, paralysing your business and giving a tremendous edge to the competition. Do you:

**Option 1:** Ask for a bit more time to re-examine the latest proposal from the union?

**Option 2:** Tell them that you do not negotiate under a threat?

**Option 3:** Suggest that you jointly take stock of the situation and see what can be done now?

### Your reactions and comments:

✎ ......................................................................
......................................................................
......................................................................
......................................................................
......................................................................
......................................................................
......................................................................
......................................................................
......................................................................
......................................................................
......................................................................

# Comments

**Option 1:** Forget it. That's not going to work. You have tried that before. Better to find something new, and better.

**Option 2:** ...and go out of business? Are you sure there is no other way?

**Option 3:** This looks ideal, but there is a good chance it is not going to work. You must give something first, then take stock. Can't you find something to concede?

# Negotiation and ambiguity

Keep in mind that any negotiation is ambiguous because:

- ✔ You do not know what the other party's position is.

- ✔ You are not sure (at least at the beginning) about your first move. *What is best?*

- ✔ You are finding your way, matching the reactions of the other party and interpreting them.

- ✔ Meanings are not in words but in people (people are different; therefore they give different meanings to the same words).

It is then important to be aware of what people's reactions are when facing ambiguity.

**Words are meaningless and... powerful**

Ambiguity triggers a well known set of emotions and behaviours in most human beings:

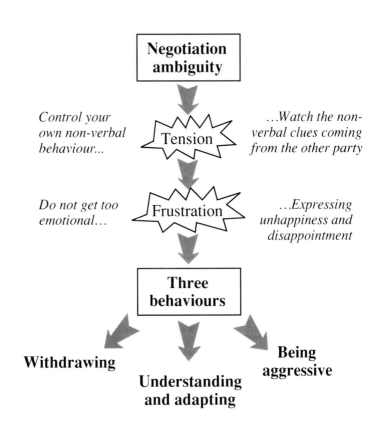

# Three negotiating lessons:

1. Do not be surprised if you see people withdrawing and attacking (fighting) while negotiating (expect those reactions).

2. Control your own reactions.

3. Decide if the ambiguity (and the emotions and behaviours it triggers) is good for you and act accordingly.

## Difficult cases in negotiation

### *Summary*

In negotiation, there are no cookbooks and no recipes. Each situation is different and requires an adaptive approach. However, a few basic principles can be applied when you encounter difficult cases:

1. Do not react too quickly and too harshly.

2. Always look for options – not one, but at least **three**.

3. Examine the pros and cons of each option, then act. Watch the reactions of your opponents carefully, and adjust accordingly.

4. Trust your intuition and check the vibrations coming from the other party.

5. Manage ambiguity.

# CHAPTER 8

## Test yourself and… enjoy!

# Three stories for one demonstration

Have a look at the following drawing and stories (one at a time) and identify what is special about the described negotiation.

When you have your answer, move to the next page, where the answer is presented.

**1.  Look at the drawing and think about what is going on.**

# Negotiating without saying anything or the power of non-verbal communication

The person who is looking at his watch is trying to influence the other negotiators. *Is it so late already? Time to stop? Shall we adjourn…?*

He could also have used a three-step gesture:

**Step 1.** Looking at the watch

**Step 2.** Expressing amazement

**Step 3.** Checking if the watch is still working

## Tips for the negotiator

- Be alert and watch out for covert signals that the other party will send you.

- Create trust through the use of your eyes (showing interest), your mouth (smiling) and your hands (open and relaxed).

- Show the other negotiator that you are genuinely interested in what he or she is saying (nodding, taking notes, making vocal sounds to encourage him or her to go on...)

## 2. Read the following story and reflect on its meaning (from a negotiation viewpoint)

An employee working in a big organization had a major problem with his boss. He did not like him, at all. As a matter of fact, he hated the manager who had mistreated him several times in the past.

However, the employee couldn't afford to say anything to his boss who was a powerful man. He needed his job and his salary to take care of his family.

But one day, he found the solution to his problem... He went to his boss's office, knocked on the door and walked towards the manager who was sitting behind his desk, and got quite close to him. He looked at him straight in the eyes and said: *"You'll never guess what happened to me ten minutes ago. I was walking in the street when a man came to me, looked at me straight in the eyes and said: you are stupid!"*. The boss looked at the employee and said: *"There are crazy people in the streets."*

# Saying something without saying it

Look at the story again:

- ✗ The employee is upset about his boss. Very upset.
- ✗ He cannot afford to say anything to the boss because he needs his job.
- ✗ He has found a way to ventilate his anger without taking any risk.
- ✗ He tells the boss... without telling anything.
- ✗ The boss's reaction: *"There are crazy people in the streets!"*.

## Tips for the negotiator

- ✌ Practice the "If... then..." tactic (no commitment).
- ✌ Use analogies *"Two years ago, in a similar negotiation, the two parties..."*
- ✌ Assume things *"Let's assume that we have solved this problem..."*

# In the same line, we also have:
## Saying something... indirectly

This is a scene from Pagnol's movie, "La Femme du Boulanger" (The Baker's Wife). The story is simple. The negotiation tool used is amazingly powerful.

- ✘ The baker's wife has left her husband.

- ✘ The baker is upset, but does not want to acknowledge that she has left the village with the shepherd. "She is visiting her mother".

- ✘ She comes back and wants to talk to him about what happened.

- ✘ He does not want to hear a word of what she has to say. "You were with your mother".

- ✘ The cat comes back after having left the house for a couple of days. The baker explodes, telling the cat what he thinks of what it did. Actually, everything he says is directed towards his wife, who understands perfectly...

## Tips for the negotiator

- ⚔ Soften your "hard" statements by addressing them to somebody else: *"In my last negotiation..."*

- ⚔ Be rhetorical: *"I am wondering if..."*

- ⚔ Talk to yourself: *"Well, I am asking myself if..."*, talk to a member of your team (aloud).

**3. Look carefully at the drawing below and get three new tips on how to negotiate effectively out of it:**

✎

1. ............................................................................

   ............................................................................

2. ............................................................................

   ............................................................................

3. ............................................................................

   ............................................................................

# Testing and... enjoying

## *Summary*

Motivated negotiators:

1. Test themselves from time to time to know more about their strengths and weaknesses and decide on how to improve their effectiveness.

2. Try out new behaviours to learn new ways to negotiate.

3. Read a lot about negotiation.

4. Challenge themselves with new questions.

5. Use daily life situations to acquire new negotiating tools.

# The essentials in one piece

## *The negotiator checklist*

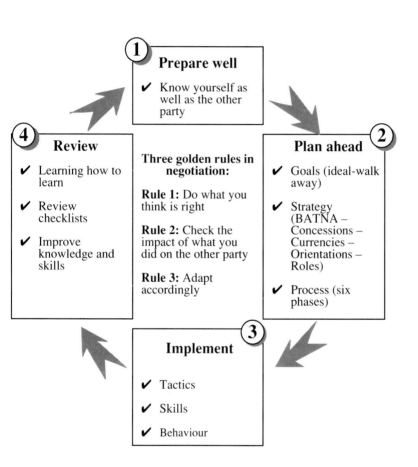

**① Prepare well**
- ✔ Know yourself as well as the other party

**② Plan ahead**
- ✔ Goals (ideal-walk away)
- ✔ Strategy (BATNA – Concessions – Currencies – Orientations – Roles)
- ✔ Process (six phases)

**③ Implement**
- ✔ Tactics
- ✔ Skills
- ✔ Behaviour

**④ Review**
- ✔ Learning how to learn
- ✔ Review checklists
- ✔ Improve knowledge and skills

**Three golden rules in negotiation:**

**Rule 1:** Do what you think is right

**Rule 2:** Check the impact of what you did on the other party

**Rule 3:** Adapt accordingly

# A reading list for the curious negotiator

ANZIEU D., *La psychologie de la négociation entre les groupes.* Louvain: Université de Louvain. 1971.

BELLENGER L., *L'argumentation.* Paris: Editions ESF. 1980.

BELLENGER L., *La négociation.* Paris: PUF. 1984.

BELLENGER L., *Les techniques d'argumentation et de négociation.* Paris: Entreprise Moderne d'Edition. 1978.

BELLENGER L., *La persuasion.* Paris: PUF. 1984.

BELLENGER L., *Etre constructif dans les négociations et les discussions.* Paris: Entreprise Moderne d'Edition. 1984.

BOURDOISEAU Y., *Savoir négocier dans la vie privée, sociale et professionnelle.* Paris: CEPE. Retz. 1976.

CALERO H.H., *Winning the Negotiation.* New York: Hawthorne Books. 1979.

CASSE P. and DEOL S.P.S., *Managing Intercultural Negotiations.* Washington D.C.: SIETAR. 1985.

COHEN H., *You Can Negotiate Anything.* New York: Bantam Books. 1980.

DERRIEN P., *Mener et réussir une négociation.* Paris: Editions d'Organisation. 1977.

DRUCKMANN D., *Negotiations.* Beverly Hills: Sage Publications. 1977.

DUPONT C., *La négociation, conduite, théorie, applications*. Paris: Collection Hommes et Entreprises. Edition Dalloz. 1986.

FISHER G., *International Negotiation – A Cross-Cultural Perspective*. Chicago: Intercultural Press. 1982.

FISHER R., and URY W., *Getting to Yes*. Boston: Houghton Mifflin Company. 1981.

HARNETT D.L. and CUMMINGS L.L., *Bargaining Behavior: An International Study*. Houston: Dame Publications. 1980.

HOLTZ H., *The Consultant's Guide to Winning Clients*. New York: John Wiley & Sons. 1988.

ILLICH J., *The Art and Skill of Successful Negotiation*. Englewood Cliffs, N.J.: Prentice-Hall. 1973.

ILLICH J., *Power Negotiating*. New York: Addison-Wesley. 1980.

JANDT F.E., *Win-Win Negotiating*. New York: John Wiley & Sons. 1985.

KAPOOR A., *Planning for International Business Negotiation*. Cambridge, MA: Bollinger Publishing Company. 1975.

KARRASS C.L., *Give and Take*. New York: Thomas Y. Crowell. 1974.

KARRASS C.L., *The Negotiating Game*. New York: Thomas Y. Crowell. 1970.

KENNEDY G., BENSON J. and McMILLAN J., *Managing Negotiations*. Englewood Cliffs, N.J.: Prentice-Hall. 1982.

LAUNAY R., *La négociation*. Paris: ESF. 1983.

LAX D.A. and SEBENIUS J.K., *The Manager as Negotiator. Bargaining for Cooperation and Competitive Gain*. New York: The Free Press. 1986.

LEBEL P., *L'art de la négociation*. Paris: Editions d'Organisation. 1984.

LE POOLE SAMFRITS, *Never Take No for an Answer. A Guide to Successful Negotiation*. London: Kogan Page. 1987.

MISSENARD B., *Savoir négocier en affaires*. Paris: Editions d'Organisation. 1973.

MISSENARD B., *Savoir négocier face-à-face*. Paris: Editions d'Organisation.

MORAN R.T., *Getting Your Yen's Worth. How to Negotiate with Japan Inc*. Houston: Gulf Publishing Company. 1985.

MUCCHIELLI R., *La dynamique des groupes*. Paris: ESF, Entreprise Moderne d'Edition. 1986.

NIERENBERG G.I., *The Art of Negotiating*. New York: Cornerstone Library. 1968.

NIERENBERG G.I., *Creative Business Negotiating*. New York: Hawthorne Books. 1971.

NIERENBERG G.I., *Fundamentals of Negotiating*. New York: Hawthorne Books. 1973.

OLERON P., *L'argumentation*. Paris. PUF.

PONSSARD J.P., *Logique de la négociation et théorie des jeux*. Paris: Editions d'organisation. 1977.

PRUITT D.G., *Negotiation Behavior*. New York: Academic Press. 1981.

TOUZARD H., *La médiation et la résolution des conflits*. Paris: PUF. 1977.

WINKLER J., *Bargaining for Results*. London: Pan Books. 1981.

# Index